Debunking Ayn Rand

The Truth About Money Creation

or

Why Work DOESN'T Create Money

By Vladimir Lincoln Armstrong

1. Table of Contents

Chapter 1: Introduction

1.1: The Influence of Ayn Rand

Ayn Rand's philosophy of Objectivism has had a significant impact on economic and political thought since the mid-20th century. Her advocacy for individualism, rational self-interest, and laissez-faire capitalism has resonated with economists, politicians, and a dedicated group of followers known as Objectivists. One of the key tenets of Rand's philosophy is the assertion that money is created by the productive efforts of individuals, particularly workers. This concept has garnered attention and sparked debate among scholars and practitioners in the field of economics. However, this assertion has also faced robust criticism and skepticism. This chapter aims to delve into the core of this claim and present a logical refutation of why Ayn Rand's assertion about money creation is fundamentally flawed.

The influence of Ayn Rand's ideas can be observed in various spheres, including academia, public policy, and popular culture. Ayn Rand's magnum opus, "Atlas Shrugged," has sold over 7 million copies since its publication in 1957, and continues to be a perennial bestseller. The novel has not only influenced a generation of readers but has also permeated into political discourse, with several high-profile public figures expressing admiration for Rand's ideas. In academia, the Ayn Rand Institute has been promoting Objectivist thought and scholarship, contributing to the perpetuation of Rand's ideas and generating discussions on her economic theories. Additionally, Objectivism has inspired the formation of political groups such as the Libertarian Party and has been cited as an influential force in shaping the economic policies of certain nations.

Despite the widespread reach of Ayn Rand's philosophy, her assertions about money creation have come under scrutiny by mainstream economists and scholars. The prevailing consensus among economists is that money creation in modern economies is a function of central banks and financial institutions, rather than the labor of individual workers. This is supported by empirical evidence showing that the majority of money in circulation is created through the process of fractional reserve banking and central bank monetary policy, rather than through the direct efforts of individual workers. Furthermore, the intricate mechanisms of money creation involve factors such as interest rates, reserve requirements, and monetary aggregates, which are not accounted for in Rand's simplistic assertion.

In the pages that follow, we will dissect Ayn Rand's claim about money creation and present a comprehensive analysis that illuminates the nuanced realities of monetary economics. By examining the historical context, theoretical frameworks, and empirical evidence, we aim to provide a rigorous and logical refutation of why Ayn Rand's assertion about money creation does not align with the fundamental principles of modern economics. Our exploration will challenge the pervasive influence of Rand's ideas on this subject and offer a compelling alternative perspective grounded in empirical reality and economic theory.

As we navigate through the intricate terrain of money creation and economic theory, it is essential to remain open-minded and receptive to critical inquiry. The overarching goal of this chapter is to stimulate thoughtful reflection and discourse on the intersection of philosophy and economics, while offering a balanced and evidence-based critique of Ayn Rand's assertion about money creation. It is through this rigorous engagement with ideas that we can advance our understanding of economic principles and contribute to the ongoing evolution of economic thought.

1.2: The Claim About Money Creation

In Ayn Rand's philosophy, she claimed that money is created by the producers and workers in society. This claim is the cornerstone of her argument that the wealth in society is created by the efforts of the individual, rather than through collective means or government intervention. However, this assertion overlook the comprehensive process of money creation, which involves variou stakeholders and mechanisms.

In reality, money creation is primarily the prerogative of central banks. According to the Federal Reserve, the central bank of the United States, new money i created through a process called "open market operations". By purchasing government securities, the central bank injects new money into the economy Additionally, through the fractional reserve banking system, commercial bank extend loans to individuals and businesses, thereby creating new money in the form of bank deposits. These deposits then circulate in the economy contributing to the overall money supply. This system effectively illustrates tha money creation is not solely derived from the efforts of workers, but also involve the actions of central banks and commercial institutions.

Furthermore, the creation of money is not limited to the physical printing o currency. In modern economies, the majority of money exists in digital form a bank deposits and electronic transfers. In the Eurozone, for instance, studies have revealed that over 90% of the money supply is in the form of bank deposits and electronic currency. This digital representation of money underscores the intricate and multifaceted nature of money creation, which goes beyond the direct efforts of workers and producers.

Moreover, the concept of "fiat money" further complicates Rand's claim. Fia money is currency that a government has declared to be legal tender, despite lacking intrinsic value. The value of fiat money is derived from the trust and confidence of the people in the issuing authority. In essence, the creation and maintenance of fiat money rests on the authority and stability of the government, rather than the labor of individuals.

n summary, Ayn Rand's assertion that money is created by the workers neglects he complex processes involved in money creation, such as central bank operations, fractional reserve banking, digital currency, and the concept of fiat money. The comprehensive understanding of money creation demonstrates that is not solely derived from the efforts of workers, but rather a multifaceted ystem involving various institutions and mechanisms. This critical analysis unveils he fallacy of Rand's claim and provides a more comprehensive perspective on he nature of money creation in modern economies.

.3: Overview of the Debunking Approach

n this section, we will provide an overview of the debunking approach we will use to refute Ayn Rand's claim that money is created by workers. Ayn Rand's perspective, outlined in her book "Atlas Shrugged," states that money is created hrough the productive labor of individuals. However, this perspective overlooks he complex mechanisms behind money creation in modern economies. Our approach will draw on economic theory, historical evidence, and empirical data to dismantle Rand's oversimplified viewpoint and offer a more accurate understanding of money creation.

o begin our debunking approach, we will delve into the foundational principles of money creation in a modern economy. This involves examining the role of central banks, commercial banks, and monetary policy in the creation and management of money supply. We will provide a comprehensive analysis of how the fractional reserve banking system facilitates the creation of broad money (M2) through the process of lending and the expansion of credit. urthermore, we will explore the quantitative easing measures implemented by central banks and their impact on the money supply, inflation, and economic tability.

In addition to dissecting the technical aspects of money creation, we will explore the historical and empirical evidence that contradicts Ayn Rand's assertion. By examining historical examples and real-world data, we will demonstrate that money creation is not solely dependent on the labor of individuals, but rather a multi-faceted process influenced by government policies, financial institutions and macroeconomic conditions. Furthermore, we will analyze the correlation between productivity, wage levels, and money supply growth to provide a nuanced understanding of the relationship between labor and money creation.

Moreover, our debunking approach will address the ideological underpinnings of Ayn Rand's perspective on money creation. We will critically evaluate the philosophical and ethical principles embedded in Rand's objectivist philosophy particularly her emphasis on individualism, rational self-interest, and the virtue of productive labor. By critically examining these principles in the context of modern economic realities, we will elucidate the limitations and misconceptions underpinning Rand's portrayal of money creation.

In conclusion, our debunking approach will utilize a multifaceted strategy encompassing economic theory, historical analysis, empirical evidence, and philosophical critique to dismantle Ayn Rand's claim that money is created by workers. By providing a comprehensive and rigorous refutation, we aim to offer a more nuanced and accurate understanding of the complex dynamics of money creation in modern economies, catering to the interests of economists, politicians, and Objectivists alike.

1.4: Target Audience and Objectives

In this section, we will discuss the target audience and objectives of this book "Debunking Ayn Rand: The Truth About Money Creation." The target audience for this book includes economists, politicians, and Objectivists who are interested in gaining a deeper understanding of the intricacies of money creation and it mpact on the economy. These individuals are likely to have a keen interest in economic theory and policy, and may have varying perspectives on the role of money in the economy.

Economists form a significant part of the target audience, as they are central to the study and understanding of money creation. According to the Bureau of Labor Statistics, the United States employed over 21,000 economists in 2020, with an expected job growth rate of 14% from 2020 to 2030. This indicates the growing relevance of this profession and the importance of staying updated with current economic literature and debates.

In addition, politicians are an essential audience for this book, as they are responsible for shaping economic policies that directly impact money creation and its consequences. According to the Congressional Research Service, there are 535 members of Congress in the United States, each playing a crucial role in formulating and implementing economic policies. It is essential for these policymakers to have a comprehensive understanding of the mechanisms behind money creation to make informed decisions that will benefit the economy and society at large.

Objectivists, followers of the philosophy of Ayn Rand, also form a significant part of the target audience. With over 25 million copies of Ayn Rand's books sold globally, her influence is widespread, and her ideas continue to shape the perspectives of many individuals. Therefore, it is crucial to engage with Objectivists and provide them with a critical analysis of Ayn Rand's views on money creation, offering alternative perspectives and insights that may challenge their beliefs.

The primary objective of this book is to logically refute Ayn Rand's claim that money is created by workers. Through rigorous analysis, empirical evidence, and

9

scholarly research, we aim to provide a comprehensive debunking of this assertion, thereby contributing to a more nuanced and accurate understanding of money creation. This refutation serves to encourage critical thinking and informed discourse among our target audience and beyond.

Furthermore, we seek to broaden the perspectives of our readers by presenting alternative theories and viewpoints on money creation that offer a more comprehensive understanding of the complex processes involved. By doing so we aim to foster an environment of intellectual curiosity and open-mindedness where individuals are receptive to considering diverse interpretations and insights.

Ultimately, the objectives of this book are aligned with the pursuit of knowledge critical thinking, and the advancement of economic literacy. By engaging with our target audience and addressing their interests and concerns, we endeavor to contribute to a more informed and enlightened discourse on the subject of money creation and its implications for the economy and society.

Chapter 2: Historical Perspectives on Money Creation

2.1: Historical Evolution of Money

The historical evolution of money is a fascinating journey that reflects the development of human civilization. Money has evolved from simple bartering systems to complex financial instruments we use today. The earliest forms of money were tangible goods such as cattle, grain, and shells, which served as a medium of exchange. These commodities were valuable because they were essential for survival and had intrinsic value. However, carrying large quantities of these goods for trade was impractical, leading to the use of precious metals as a medium of exchange. The use of precious metals as money, such as gold and silver, allowed for easier trade and became the standard for centuries.

As societies became more advanced, the need for a more efficient medium of exchange led to the development of coinage. The advent of coins standardized the value of money and facilitated trade across regions and cultures. The use of coins also allowed for the accumulation of wealth and the development of complex economic systems. The concept of representative money, in the form of banknotes and promissory notes, further revolutionized the monetary system. These forms of currency represented a claim on a commodity, usually gold or silver, stored in a secure location, introducing the concept of fiat money backed by a reserve.

The evolution of money continued with the establishment of centralized banking systems and the issuance of paper currency by governments. This shift from commodity-backed money to fiat currency marked a significant turning point in the history of money creation. The ability of governments to create money out of thin air, without the need for tangible assets to back it up, changed the dynamics of the monetary system. This transition has led to debates about the

implications of unlimited money creation and its impact on inflation, monetar
policy, and the stability of financial systems.

The historical evolution of money also reflects the role of central banks i
regulating and controlling the money supply. Central banks play a crucial role i
influencing interest rates, managing inflation, and stabilizing the econom
through monetary policy tools. The creation of money, through mechanisms suc
as open market operations and reserve requirements, allows central banks t
adjust the money supply based on economic conditions.

In conclusion, the historical evolution of money has undergone significar
transformations, from bartering and commodity-based systems to modern fic
currencies. Understanding the historical context of money creation provide
valuable insights into the complexities of the financial system and the
implications of different monetary policies. It is essential to recognize the
historical factors that have shaped the current monetary landscape to assess the
validity of various theories, including Ayn Rand's perspective on money creation.

2.2: Monetary Systems and Government Intervention

In exploring historical perspectives on money creation, it is essential to examine
the relationship between monetary systems and government intervention
Throughout history, governments have played a significant role in shaping and
regulating monetary systems, often in response to economic challenges and the
need to stabilize financial markets. One of the earliest forms of governmen
intervention in monetary systems can be found in ancient civilizations, where
rulers issued coins as a means of standardizing and controlling the money supply
For example, the Roman Empire implemented a standardized currency system t
facilitate trade and taxation, exerting central control over money creation and
circulation.

Moving forward in history, the role of government intervention in monetary systems became more pronounced during the emergence of central banks. The establishment of central banks, such as the Bank of England in 1694, marked a pivotal moment in the evolution of monetary systems and government intervention. Central banks were created with the primary objective of regulating the money supply, managing interest rates, and providing financial stability. These institutions became key players in the process of money creation, as they gained the authority to issue and control the circulation of currency.

The 20th century witnessed a significant shift in the relationship between monetary systems and government intervention, particularly during periods of economic upheaval such as the Great Depression. In response to the financial crisis, governments around the world intervened by implementing monetary policies aimed at stimulating economic growth and stabilizing the banking sector. For instance, the New Deal in the United States under President Franklin D. Roosevelt included measures to regulate the banking system, expand public works projects, and introduce social welfare programs. These interventions aimed to address the shortcomings of unregulated capitalism and alleviate the impact of the economic downturn.

Furthermore, the Bretton Woods Agreement of 1944 established a new framework for international monetary cooperation, laying the foundation for the creation of the International Monetary Fund (IMF) and the World Bank. The agreement aimed to promote exchange rate stability and prevent competitive currency devaluations, demonstrating the increasing influence of government intervention in shaping global monetary systems.

In contemporary times, government intervention in monetary systems remains a crucial aspect of economic policymaking. Central banks, such as the Federal Reserve in the United States and the European Central Bank, continue to play a pivotal role in regulating money creation through mechanisms such as oper market operations and setting reserve requirements for financial institutions Additionally, the implementation of fiscal policies, including governmen spending and taxation, contributes to the overall management of money supply and economic stability.

Overall, historical perspectives on monetary systems underscore the pervasive impact of government intervention in shaping money creation and maintaining financial stability. The evolution of monetary systems has been intricately linked to the development of regulatory frameworks and institutions designed to oversee the process of money creation, reflecting the dynamic interplay between government intervention and economic dynamics.

2.3: The Role of Central Banks

In understanding the historical perspectives on money creation, it is essential to delve into the pivotal role played by central banks. Central banks are the cornerstone of modern monetary systems and have a profound impact on the creation and regulation of money. The role of central banks in money creation i particularly significant in influencing interest rates, controlling inflation, and maintaining financial stability within an economy.

Central banks have the authority to issue currency and regulate the money supply. Through the process of open market operations, central banks can directly influence the money supply by buying or selling government securities This mechanism allows central banks to inject liquidity into the financial system or withdraw it, thereby impacting the overall money supply. For instance, the Federal Reserve in the United States adjusts the federal funds rate to influence the money supply, which in turn affects economic activity and price levels

Central banks also play a pivotal role in safeguarding the stability of the financic system. They act as lenders of last resort, providing emergency funds to financial institutions during times of crisis to prevent widespread financial panics and systemic collapses. This function was exemplified during the 2008 financial crisis, where central banks around the world implemented various measures, such as quantitative easing, to stabilize financial markets and support economic recovery.

Furthermore, central banks are instrumental in managing inflation and price stability. By setting benchmark interest rates and implementing monetary policy tools, central banks aim to achieve their inflation targets, ensuring that the purchasing power of money remains relatively stable over time. For example, the European Central Bank targets an inflation rate of close to, but below, 2% over the medium term, as part of its monetary policy strategy to maintain price stability within the Eurozone.

It is important to note that the role and functions of central banks vary across different countries. For instance, some central banks, such as the Bank of England, have been granted operational independence to set monetary policy, free from government influence, in order to maintain credibility and build public trust. In contrast, central banks in some emerging economies may face challenges in maintaining their independence due to political and economic constraints.

In conclusion, the role of central banks in money creation cannot be overstated. Their influence extends to the control of the money supply, regulation of interest rates, maintenance of financial stability, and management of inflation. Understanding the functions and policies of central banks is crucial in comprehending the dynamics of money creation and its impact on the economy. As such, a thorough examination of the historical and contemporary roles of central banks provides valuable insights into the broader discussions on money creation and economic policy.

2.4: Case Studies in Money Creation

In examining historical case studies of money creation, it is essential to evaluate the diverse ways in which monetary systems have evolved and the impact they have had on economies. One notable case study is the Weimar Republic in post-World War I Germany, which experienced hyperinflation due to the excessive printing of money. This extreme scenario serves as a cautionary tale about the consequences of uncontrolled money creation and the necessity of responsible monetary policies. Another case study is the United States during the Great Depression, where the Federal Reserve's contraction of the money supply exacerbated the economic downturn, highlighting the significance of balancing money creation with economic stability.

Furthermore, the implementation of quantitative easing in the aftermath of the 2008 financial crisis provides a more recent case study in money creation. The Federal Reserve and other central banks utilized this unconventional monetary policy to inject liquidity into the financial system and stimulate economic activity. This approach raised important questions about the potential long-term impacts of expanding the money supply and the trade-offs between short-term relief and future inflationary pressures.

Looking at these case studies through the lens of Ayn Rand's assertion about money creation, it becomes evident that money is not simply a product of individual labor, as she argued. Instead, it is the product of a complex interplay of factors, including government policies, central bank actions, and market forces. These case studies underscore the necessity of a nuanced understanding of money creation and the recognition that it is a multifaceted process that influences economic outcomes on a global scale.

In conclusion, historical case studies of money creation serve as valuable sources of insight into the complexities of monetary systems and their profound effects on societies. Analyzing these cases enables economists, politicians, and Objectivists to appreciate the intricacies of money creation beyond Ayn Rand's oversimplified assertion. By critically examining these real-world examples, we gain a deeper understanding of the factors that shape monetary policies and their implications for economies, offering valuable lessons for informed decision-making and policy formulation.

Chapter 3: The Mechanisms of Money Creation

3.1: Understanding the Creation of Fiat Currency

In order to debunk Ayn Rand's claim about money creation, it's essential to understand the mechanisms behind the creation of fiat currency. Fiat currency is a form of money that is not backed by a physical commodity such as gold or silver, but rather by the issuing government's decree or law. The process of creating fiat currency is primarily conducted by central banks, which are responsible for managing a country's monetary policy and issuing currency. Central banks have the authority to create new money through a mechanism called "open market operations," which involves the buying and selling of government securities such as treasury bills and bonds.

When a central bank wants to increase the money supply, it purchases government securities from banks and other financial institutions. In return, the central bank credits the accounts of the sellers with newly created reserves, effectively injecting new money into the financial system. Conversely, when the central bank wants to decrease the money supply, it sells government securities, thereby reducing the reserves of commercial banks and limiting their ability to lend and create new money. This process gives central banks significant control over the quantity of money in the economy, allowing them to influence interest rates and regulate economic activity.

Furthermore, the creation of fiat currency is closely linked to the concept of fractional reserve banking, which enables commercial banks to create money through the lending process. When a bank issues a loan, it does not need to hold the full amount of the loan in reserves; instead, it is only required to hold a fraction of the loan amount as reserves. This means that banks have the ability to "create" money by effectively expanding the money supply through lending activities. For example, if a bank lends $100 to a borrower, it can then count that

$100 loan as an asset on its balance sheet, even though the actual physical currency only exists as a deposit in the borrower's account. This process is known as "money creation through credit extension" and plays a significant role in increasing the overall money supply in the economy.

It is important to note that the creation of fiat currency and the expansion of the money supply through fractional reserve banking are regulated and supervised by central banks and government authorities to maintain stability in the financial system. However, this mechanism of money creation stands in stark contrast to Ayn Rand's assertion that money is created by workers through their production and trade. In reality, the creation of fiat currency is a complex process that involves the coordination of central banks, commercial banks, and government institutions, and it is closely tied to monetary policy and financial regulations.

In conclusion, understanding the creation of fiat currency is crucial for debunking Ayn Rand's claim about money creation. The process involves the issuance of new money by central banks through open market operations, as well as the expansion of the money supply through the lending activities of commercial banks. By grasping the intricacies of money creation, economists, politicians, and Objectivists can gain a more comprehensive understanding of the modern monetary system and its role in the economy.

3.2: The Relationship Between Production and Money Creation

In order to understand the relationship between production and money creation, it is crucial to first grasp the fundamental mechanisms of money creation. Contrary to Ayn Rand's assertion that money is created by workers, money creation primarily occurs through the process of banking and lending. When a bank makes a loan, it essentially creates new money by extending credit to borrowers. This newly created money enters circulation and contributes to the overall money supply in the economy. In addition, central banks play a pivotal role in money creation through open market operations and the setting of interest rates, which influence the lending activities of commercial banks and consequently impact the quantity of money in the economy.

The relationship between production and money creation is intrinsically linked to the concept of value creation. Production, in the economic sense, involves the transformation of inputs into goods and services that are valued by consumers. This creation of value contributes to overall economic output and wealth generation within an economy. As production increases, through innovation, technological advancements, and enhanced productivity, the potential for value creation expands, leading to an increase in the demand for labor, resources, and capital. This, in turn, can influence the demand for credit and the supply of money in the economy. Therefore, the relationship between production and money creation can be viewed as a dynamic interplay between the real economy and the financial system.

Moreover, it is essential to recognize that while production lays the foundation for economic activity, the mechanisms of money creation operate within a broader macroeconomic context. The quantity theory of money posits a direct relationship between the quantity of money in an economy and the price level, assuming that the velocity of money and the level of real output remain constant. This theory underscores the impact of money creation on inflation and economic stability, highlighting the critical role of central banks in managing the money supply to maintain price stability and sustainable economic growth.

Furthermore, the relationship between production and money creation is underscored by the concept of financial intermediation. Financial institutions such as banks, facilitate the allocation of capital from savers to borrowers, allowing funds to flow to productive investments and initiatives. This intermediation process connects the real economy with the financial sector, nfluencing the availability of credit for businesses and entrepreneurs seeking to expand production and create value. Therefore, the dynamics of money creation are inextricably intertwined with the productive activities that drive economic growth and development.

n summary, the relationship between production and money creation encompasses the dynamics of value creation, the macroeconomic implications of money supply, and the role of financial intermediaries in resource allocation. By understanding these intricate linkages, economists, politicians, and Objectivists can gain a comprehensive perspective on the interplay between production and money creation, debunking Ayn Rand's oversimplified assertion and embracing a more nuanced understanding of the complex mechanisms shaping modern economies.

3.3: The Influence of Financial Institutions

The influence of financial institutions on the creation of money is a crucial aspect of understanding the mechanisms behind money creation. Financial institutions play a significant role in the money creation process through their lending and investment activities. When considering the influence of financial institutions on money creation, it is essential to delve into the concept of fractional reserve banking. This system allows banks to lend out a larger sum of money than the actual deposits they hold, thereby effectively creating money through the process of lending. For example, if a bank has $100 in deposits and a reserve requirement of 10%, it can lend out $90 while still retaining $10 as a reserve. As a result, the original $100 deposit and the newly created $90 loan amount to a total of $190 in the money supply, highlighting the significant impact of financial institutions on money creation.

Moreover, the actions of central banks also exert a profound influence on the money creation process. Central banks have the authority to control the money supply by regulating the reserve requirements of commercial banks and by engaging in open market operations. Through open market operations, central banks buy or sell government securities, affecting the reserves of commercial banks. By adjusting the reserve requirements and conducting open market operations, central banks can influence the ability of commercial banks to create money through lending and investment. For example, by lowering the reserve requirements, central banks can encourage commercial banks to lend more, thereby increasing the money supply. On the other hand, by selling government securities, central banks can reduce the reserves of commercial banks, constraining their ability to create money.

Furthermore, the influence of financial institutions on money creation extends to the realm of investment and capital markets. Financial institutions such as investment banks and hedge funds play a crucial role in allocating resources and capital, thereby influencing the overall money supply and economic activity. Their investment decisions can impact the flow of funds throughout the economy, affecting the availability of credit and liquidity. For instance investment banks facilitate the issuance of corporate bonds and the underwriting of stock offerings, which directly impact the amount of money available for investment and business expansion.

In conclusion, the influence of financial institutions on money creation is multifaceted and encompasses aspects such as fractional reserve banking central bank policies, and investment activities. It is essential to recognize the intricate interplay between financial institutions and the money creation process to gain a comprehensive understanding of the dynamics at play. By comprehending the influence of financial institutions, economists, politicians and Objectivists can better evaluate and critique Ayn Rand's assertions regarding the origins of money.

3.4: Money Creation and Economic Policy

n understanding the mechanisms of money creation, it is imperative to delve nto the role of economic policy in shaping the process. Economic policy refers o the actions that governments take in the economic field. These actions can encompass fiscal policy, monetary policy, and regulatory policy, all of which have significant impacts on money creation.

iscal policy, which involves government spending and taxation, influences money creation through its effect on the overall economy. For instance, when he government increases its spending, it injects more money into the economy, eading to an expansion of the money supply. On the other hand, when taxes are increased, it can reduce disposable income and subsequently limit pending, thus affecting the pace of money creation.

Monetary policy, managed by central banks, has a notable influence on money creation. By setting interest rates and controlling the money supply, central banks can alter the availability of credit in the economy, which in turn affects he speed and volume of money creation. For example, in response to economic conditions, central banks can adjust interest rates to encourage or discourage borrowing, subsequently impacting the money creation process.

Furthermore, regulatory policy plays a crucial role in money creation by shaping he environment in which financial institutions operate. Regulations governing banking activities, such as reserve requirements and capital adequacy ratios, directly impact the ability of banks to create money through the issuance of oans and credit. Additionally, regulations aimed at promoting financial stability and consumer protection can influence the behavior of financial institutions and borrowers, subsequently shaping the dynamics of money creation.

 is essential to note that the relationship between economic policy and money creation is complex and multifaceted. Various economic theories and model provide insights into this relationship, guiding policymakers in their decision making processes. For instance, the monetarist school of thought, popularized b economists like Milton Friedman, emphasizes the vital role of monetary policy ir controlling the money supply and stabilizing the economy. On the other hanc Keynesian economics highlights the significance of fiscal policy in managing aggregate demand and economic output, thereby influencing money creatior dynamics.

Moreover, the implementation of economic policy is subject to empirical analysi and evaluation. Through extensive data collection and econometric modeling researchers and policymakers assess the impacts of specific policy measures on money creation and broader economic variables. This empirical evidence serve as a foundation for refining and adjusting economic policies to achieve desirec outcomes in terms of money creation, inflation, employment, and economic growth.

In conclusion, the interplay between economic policy and money creation is critical area of study for economists, policymakers, and financial analysts Understanding the intricate connections between fiscal policy, monetary policy and regulatory policy is essential for comprehending the dynamics of mone creation and its implications for the overall economy. By examining the quantitative impacts of various policy measures and drawing on economic theories, stakeholders can navigate the complexities of money creation anc contribute to informed and effective policy decisions.

Chapter 4: Ayn Rand's Perspective on Money Creation

4.1: Analyzing Ayn Rand's Philosophical Framework

In order to critically evaluate Ayn Rand's perspective on money creation, it is essential to delve into her broader philosophical framework. Ayn Rand, a prominent figure in the world of Objectivism, advocated for a philosophy centered around rational self-interest, individualism, and laissez-faire capitalism. Within this framework, Rand argued that the creation of wealth and value originates from the productive efforts of individuals who engage in entrepreneurial pursuits and create goods and services. She vehemently opposed government intervention in economic matters and championed the free market as the most efficient allocator of resources. Rand's views on money creation are deeply intertwined with these core beliefs, as she advocated for the idea that money is created through the productive labor and innovations of individuals in society.

Rand's philosophical framework often stands at odds with conventional economic theories, particularly in the realm of money creation. Classical economic theories, as supported by leading economists, argue that money creation is a function of the banking system and the central bank's monetary policy. According to these theories, money is created through the process of fractional reserve banking, whereby commercial banks are able to lend out a multiple of the deposits they hold. Additionally, central banks play a pivotal role in the creation of money through open market operations and setting interest rates. These mechanisms directly impact the money supply within an economy, affecting inflation, interest rates, and overall economic activity.

When analyzing Ayn Rand's perspective on money creation, it becomes apparent that her philosophical framework does not fully align with the empirical evidence and economic realities. While it is true that individual efforts and entrepreneurship contribute to economic growth and wealth creation, the process of money creation is intricately tied to the actions of central banks and the banking system. In modern economies, the majority of the money supply is created through the extension of credit by commercial banks, underpinned by regulatory frameworks and central bank policies. These dynamics underscore the complex interplay between individual agency and systemic factors in the creation of money within an economy.

Moreover, Ayn Rand's emphasis on individual productivity as the sole driver of money creation neglects the broader macroeconomic factors that influence monetary dynamics. In reality, money creation is a multifaceted process influenced by factors such as government fiscal policy, international trade, and monetary policy. The intricate web of interactions within the global financial system further complicates the simplistic notion that money creation is solely a product of individual labor and productivity.

In conclusion, Ayn Rand's philosophical framework provides a thought-provoking perspective on money creation, emphasizing individual productivity and laissez faire capitalism. However, a comprehensive analysis reveals that her views do not fully encapsulate the complexities of modern monetary systems and the role of central banks in money creation. By critically evaluating Rand's perspective within the broader economic context, it becomes evident that a nuanced understanding of money creation necessitates consideration of both individual agency and systemic economic forces.

4.2: Examining the Role of Labor in Money Creation

In Ayn Rand's perspective, the role of labor in money creation is a central tenet of her philosophy. According to Rand, money is created through the efforts and productivity of workers. This belief is rooted in the idea that individuals who work and produce goods and services are the ones responsible for generating wealth and subsequently creating money. Rand's Objectivist philosophy emphasizes the value of human labor and how it contributes to economic growth and prosperity.

However, it's important to critically examine Ayn Rand's perspective on the role of labor in money creation. While it is true that labor is a critical component of economic activity and wealth creation, the process of money creation involves more complex mechanisms than just the efforts of individual workers. In modern economies, money creation is primarily the function of central banks through the process of monetary policy and open market operations.

Central banks, such as the Federal Reserve in the United States, have the authority to control the money supply and influence the level of economic activity through various monetary tools. One of the key mechanisms through which money is created is the process of fractional reserve banking, where banks are able to lend out a portion of the deposits they receive, effectively creating new money in the form of credit. This process is not solely dependent on the labor of individuals, but rather on the regulatory and operational functions of the banking and financial system.

Furthermore, the role of technology and automation in modern production processes cannot be overlooked. The advent of industrial and technological advancements has significantly altered the nature of labor and its relationship to wealth creation. Automation, robotics, and innovation have revolutionized the way goods and services are produced, leading to increased productivity and economic output. As a result, the traditional labor-centric view of money creation espoused by Ayn Rand may not fully capture the dynamics of the modern economy.

In addition, the global interconnectedness of economies and the role of international trade further complicates the simplistic notion of labor as the sole source of money creation. The exchange of goods and services across borders the impact of foreign exchange markets, and the role of multinational corporations all contribute to the creation and circulation of money in ways that extend beyond the scope of individual labor efforts.

In conclusion, while Ayn Rand's perspective on the role of labor in money creation underscores the importance of individual productivity and contribution to economic prosperity, a comprehensive understanding of modern monetary systems and economic dynamics requires a more nuanced approach. Money creation involves a complex interplay of central bank policies, financial regulations, technological advancements, and global economic forces that go beyond the traditional labor-centric viewpoint. By critically examining these factors, economists, politicians, and Objectivists can gain a more comprehensive understanding of the multifaceted nature of money creation in today's global economy.

4.3: Critique of Ayn Rand's Views on Money

In critiquing Ayn Rand's views on money creation, it is important to note her perspective that money is created by workers through their productive efforts Rand emphasizes the significance of individual labor and effort in creating value which is then exchanged for money. While this viewpoint acknowledges the importance of hard work and productivity, it overlooks the broader mechanisms of money creation within the modern economy.

Ayn Rand's perspective tends to oversimplify the complex process of money creation within the economy. In reality, the creation of money involves a multifaceted system that extends beyond individual labor. The modern monetary system involves the central bank, commercial banks, and various financial institutions that play a crucial role in money creation through mechanisms such as fractional reserve banking and monetary policy. According to the Bank of England, over 97% of the money supply is created by commercial banks when they make loans, rather than being directly created by the efforts of individual workers. This indicates that the process of money creation is heavily influenced by the actions and decisions of financial institutions and policymakers, rather than solely by individual labor.

Furthermore, Ayn Rand's perspective on money creation does not account for the role of government and fiscal policy in shaping the money supply. Government expenditure, taxation, and borrowing are key factors that influence the quantity of money in circulation. For instance, government spending injects money into the economy, while taxation removes money from circulation. Additionally, government borrowing affects the money supply by absorbing resources that could otherwise be available for private investment and consumption. These aspects highlight the significant influence of government and policy decisions in shaping the money creation process, challenging Rand's emphasis on individual labor as the primary source of money creation.

Moreover, Ayn Rand's focus on individual labor as the sole creator of money overlooks the role of innovation, technology, and entrepreneurship in driving economic growth and creating wealth. In a dynamic economy, advancements in technology and innovation contribute to productivity gains and economic expansion, leading to the creation of wealth and financial resources. Entrepreneurship also plays a vital role in creating value and wealth through the introduction of new products, services, and business models. These factors demonstrate that money creation is not solely dependent on individual labor but is also influenced by a broader spectrum of economic activities and innovations.

In conclusion, while Ayn Rand's emphasis on individual labor and productivity in creating value is commendable, her perspective on money creation overlooks the multifaceted processes that shape the modern monetary system. Money creation involves the actions of central banks, commercial banks, government policies, as well as technological innovation and entrepreneurship, all of which contribute to the expansion and regulation of the money supply. By recognizing the broader mechanisms of money creation, economists, policymakers, and Objectivists can gain a more comprehensive understanding of the intricate dynamics that underpin the modern monetary system.

4.4: Impact of Ayn Rand's Ideas on Economic Discourse

Ayn Rand's ideas have significantly impacted economic discourse, particularly in the realms of capitalism, individualism, and money creation. Rand's promotion of laissez-faire capitalism and her emphasis on the value of the individual have been widely influential in shaping economic and political thought. The impact of Ayn Rand's ideas on economic discourse can be seen in various areas, including public policies, academic research, and popular culture.

One of the most notable impacts of Ayn Rand's ideas has been on public policies and political ideologies. Her advocacy for individualism and free-market capitalism has influenced a number of political figures and policies. For example, Rand's ideas have been cited as influential in the development of conservative and libertarian economic policies in the United States and other countries. The concept of minimal government intervention and the free market, promoted by Rand, has been embraced by many politicians and policymakers.

In academic research, Ayn Rand's ideas have sparked extensive debate and analysis. Economists and scholars have engaged with Rand's theories on capitalism, individualism, and money creation, contributing to the development of economic thought. While some researchers have critiqued Rand's ideas, others have explored and expanded upon her theories. This has led to a rich body of literature that reflects the enduring influence of Ayn Rand on economic discourse.

Furthermore, Ayn Rand's impact on popular culture cannot be overlooked. Her novels, particularly "Atlas Shrugged" and "The Fountainhead," have attained iconic status and continue to attract readers and enthusiasts. Through her fiction, Rand popularized her philosophical and economic ideas, reaching a broad audience and shaping popular perceptions of capitalism and money creation. The enduring popularity of Rand's works indicates the lasting impact of her ideas on economic discourse.

In summary, Ayn Rand's ideas have had a profound impact on economic discourse, influencing public policies, academic research, and popular culture. Her advocacy for laissez-faire capitalism and individualism has shaped political ideologies and economic policies, while also sparking extensive debate and analysis in academic circles. Additionally, her novels have played a significant role in popularizing her ideas, contributing to their enduring influence on economic discourse.

It is essential to critically evaluate Ayn Rand's ideas in the context of economic discourse, considering both their impact and the various perspectives they have inspired. By engaging with her ideas and their influence on economic thought, economists, policymakers, and Objectivists can gain a comprehensive understanding of the complexities of money creation and its broader implications. A balanced examination of Ayn Rand's impact on economic discourse can provide valuable insights for advancing economic theory and informing policy decisions.

Chapter 5: The Reality of Money Creation

5.1: Metaphorical versus Actual Money Creation

Ayn Rand's assertion that money is created by workers is a popular metaphor but it does not accurately reflect the reality of money creation. To understand the truth about money creation, it is essential to differentiate between metaphorical and actual money creation processes.

In reality, the creation of money is not dependent on the physical labor of workers. Money is primarily created through the process of fractional reserve banking, where commercial banks are able to create money by lending out a portion of the deposits they receive. This process is regulated by central banks which set reserve requirements and control the money supply through monetary policy. According to the Federal Reserve Bank of St. Louis, commercial banks in the United States created around 93% of the total money supply through this process, as of December 2020.

Furthermore, the creation of money is also influenced by government fiscal policy, where the central government can inject money into the economy through spending or remove money from circulation through taxation. The relationship between the government's fiscal policy and the central bank's monetary policy plays a significant role in shaping the money supply and influencing economic activity.

It is important to recognize that the creation of money is a complex and multifaceted process that goes beyond the simple metaphor of workers creating money. While workers' productivity and economic activity are crucial for the overall health of the economy, the actual creation of money involves intricate interactions between commercial banks, central banks, government fiscal policy, and market forces.

n conclusion, while Ayn Rand's metaphorical claim that workers create money carries emotional and rhetorical weight, the reality of money creation involves a sophisticated interplay of banking, government policy, and market dynamics. Understanding the complexities of money creation is crucial for economists, politicians, and Objectivists to have a comprehensive grasp of the financial system and its impact on society.

5.2: The Interplay Between Labor and Monetary Systems

n the debate over the creation of money, Ayn Rand's assertion that workers are the creators of wealth has been a controversial topic. However, when delving into the interplay between labor and monetary systems, it becomes evident that the reality of money creation is far more complex than Rand's assertion suggests. n reality, money creation involves a multifaceted interplay between labor, financial institutions, and central banks.

At the core of the interplay between labor and monetary systems is the process of money creation through the banking system. When individuals or businesses take out loans from banks, new money is effectively created. This process, known as fractional reserve banking, allows banks to lend out more money than they actually hold in reserves. As a result, the act of borrowing and lending contributes to the expansion of the money supply. It is important to note that this expansion of the money supply is not solely contingent on the labor of individuals, but rather on the financial activities within the banking system.

Moreover, the role of central banks in the creation of money cannot be overlooked. Central banks play a pivotal role in controlling the money supply and influencing interest rates, thereby impacting the overall economic landscape. Through monetary policy tools such as open market operations and reserve requirements, central banks have the ability to alter the amount of money in circulation. This authority over the money supply highlights the significant influence of central banks in the creation and regulation of money extending beyond the scope of individual labor.

Additionally, the relationship between labor and money creation extends to the broader economic context. Productivity, innovation, and entrepreneurial activity all contribute to economic growth, which in turn influences the demand for money within an economy. The interconnected nature of labor, economic output, and the demand for money underscores the complexity of money creation and dispels the notion that money creation is solely derived from the labor of individuals.

Furthermore, the dynamics of international trade and global financial markets add another layer of complexity to the interplay between labor and monetary systems. The exchange of goods and services on a global scale, as well as the fluctuations in currency exchange rates, significantly impact the creation and flow of money within the global economy. The interconnectedness of labor with international trade and financial markets further underscores the intricate nature of money creation, transcending the narrow focus on individual labor as the sole creator of money.

In conclusion, when exploring the interplay between labor and monetary systems, it becomes evident that money creation is a multifaceted process influenced by a myriad of factors including financial institutions, central banks, economic productivity, and global trade. The oversimplification of money creation as solely derived from individual labor overlooks the intricate and interconnected dynamics at play in the modern financial landscape. As such, a comprehensive understanding of money creation necessitates a nuanced perspective that encompasses the broader economic and financial complexities that shape the modern monetary system.

5.3: Unpacking the Complexities of Money Creation

In unpacking the complexities of money creation, it is crucial to dispel the misconception that money is simply created by workers. Ayn Rand's assertion that money is a product of individual effort fails to capture the intricate mechanisms of modern monetary systems. In reality, money creation involves a sophisticated interplay between central banks, commercial banks, and the broader economy.

Central to the understanding of money creation is the concept of fractional reserve banking. Commercial banks are only required to hold a fraction of their deposits as reserves, allowing them to lend out the majority of deposited funds. This process of lending creates new money in the economy. According to the Federal Reserve, the M2 money supply in the United States stood at approximately $20 trillion in 2021, signifying the immense scale of money creation facilitated by the banking system.

Moreover, the central bank plays a pivotal role in money creation through open market operations and the setting of interest rates. By purchasing government securities in the open market, central banks inject funds into the banking system, expanding the money supply. Additionally, the manipulation of interest rates influences the propensity of banks to create loans, thereby impacting the overall availability of money in the economy.

Furthermore, the intricate relationship between money creation and economic stability must be examined. The expansion of the money supply can fuel economic growth by providing the necessary liquidity for investment and consumption. However, an excessive increase in the money supply can lead to inflationary pressures, eroding the purchasing power of currency. According to the International Monetary Fund, the global average inflation rate was approximately 3.2% in 2020, underscoring the potential repercussions of unchecked money creation.

In conclusion, unraveling the complexities of money creation reveals a multifaceted process that extends far beyond the labor of individuals. From fractional reserve banking to the influence of central bank policies, the creation of money is intricately intertwined with the functioning of modern economies. As economists, politicians, and Objectivists engage in discussions about money creation, it is imperative to embrace a comprehensive understanding of the mechanisms at play, transcending simplistic notions of individual labor as the sole driver of monetary expansion.

5.4: The Role of Innovation and Technological Progress in Money Creation

In the context of money creation, the role of innovation and technological progress cannot be overstated. A fundamental aspect of money creation is the increase in productivity and efficiency that comes with technological advancements and innovation. When technological progress occurs, it allows workers to produce more output with the same amount of input, which in turn leads to an increase in the overall wealth and production of a society. This increase in wealth and production has a direct impact on the creation of money.

One key way in which innovation and technological progress contribute to the creation of money is through economic growth. As new technologies are developed and implemented, they often lead to increased economic output and productivity. This, in turn, leads to overall economic growth, which can result in an increase in the money supply. For example, a study by the McKinsey Global Institute found that the adoption of digital technologies could increase global GDP by $13 trillion by 2030, thus demonstrating the significant impact of technological progress on economic growth and, by extension, money creation.

urthermore, innovation and technological progress also play a crucial role in haping the financial system and the way money is created. The development of new financial technologies, such as blockchain and digital currencies, is ransforming the way money is created, stored, and transacted. For instance, the se of cryptocurrencies has led to new forms of money creation outside raditional banking systems, thus illustrating the profound impact of technological orogress on the creation of money.

Moreover, innovation and technological progress contribute to the creation of money by fostering entrepreneurship and the development of new industries. As new technologies emerge, they create new opportunities for entrepreneurs to develop innovative products and services, leading to the growth of new ndustries and economic sectors. This, in turn, results in the creation of new wealth and the generation of additional monetary transactions, ultimately contributing o the overall creation of money in the economy.

n conclusion, the role of innovation and technological progress in money creation is significant and multifaceted. From driving economic growth to haping the financial system and fostering entrepreneurship, technological advancements play a crucial role in the creation of money. Understanding and acknowledging the impact of innovation on money creation is essential for gaining a comprehensive understanding of the dynamics of the modern economy and financial system.

Chapter 6: Conclusion and Implications

6.1: Summarizing the Debunking Arguments

In this section, we will summarize the debunking arguments presented in thi book and highlight the key points that challenge Ayn Rand's claim that money i created by workers. Throughout this book, we have meticulously examined the processes and mechanisms behind money creation to provide a logicc refutation of Rand's assertion. Our analysis has revealed the intricate interpla between central banks, commercial banks, and the wider economy in the creation of money.

Firstly, we dissected the role of central banks in money creation, emphasizing their ability to influence the money supply through open market operations discount rates, and reserve requirements. By controlling these levers, centro banks can significantly impact the quantity of money in circulatior contradicting Rand's premise that workers are the sole creators of money.

Secondly, we delved into the fractional reserve banking system, illustrating hov commercial banks are able to create money through the process of lending Through this mechanism, banks can expand the money supply beyond the actual reserves held, demonstrating that money creation is not solely derivec from the labor of workers.

Moreover, our exploration of quantitative easing and the modern monetar system highlighted the complexities of money creation in the contemporar economic landscape. The expansion of central bank balance sheets and the creation of new money to purchase assets further illuminate the multifacetec nature of money creation, dispelling the notion that it stems exclusively from the efforts of workers.

Furthermore, we expounded on the impact of technological advancements and digital currencies, underscoring the evolving nature of money creation in the digital age. The proliferation of cryptocurrencies and the potential disruption they pose to traditional banking systems underscore the need to reevaluate conventional perspectives on money creation.

In conclusion, our comprehensive examination of money creation has substantiated the fallacy in Ayn Rand's assertion that workers are the primary creators of money. By elucidating the pivotal roles played by central banks, commercial banks, and the broader economic environment, we have demonstrated that money creation is a multifaceted process influenced by a multitude of factors beyond individual labor. As economists, politicians, and Objectivists, it is imperative to embrace a nuanced understanding of money creation that transcends oversimplified assertions, and this book serves as a compelling rebuttal to Ayn Rand's flawed premise.

5.2: Implications for Economic Theory and Policy

The debunking of Ayn Rand's assertion that money is created by workers has significant implications for economic theory and policy. By understanding the true nature of money creation, economists, politicians, and Objectivists can make more informed decisions and shape effective economic policies.

First and foremost, debunking Ayn Rand's claim sheds light on the role of central banks in money creation. Contrary to Rand's assertion, money creation is not solely reliant on the efforts of workers. Rather, central banks play a crucial role in the creation and regulation of money within an economy. Through activities such as open market operations and setting interest rates, central banks influence the money supply, impacting inflation, interest rates, and overall economic activity. This recognition prompts a reevaluation of the significance of central banks in economic theory and policy formulation.

Moreover, the debunking of Ayn Rand's claim has implications for the understanding of income distribution and wealth inequality. If money creation does not solely stem from the labor of workers, it challenges the notion that wealth is equitably distributed based on individual effort. Instead, it underscore the importance of examining systemic factors, such as monetary policy and financial regulations, in shaping income distribution and wealth concentration. A deeper understanding of these dynamics can inform policy interventions aimed at addressing economic disparities and promoting inclusive growth.

Furthermore, this revelation prompts a reexamination of the impact of monetary policy on economic stability and growth. With a clearer understanding of the mechanisms of money creation, policymakers can formulate more precise monetary policies designed to achieve stable prices, maximum employment and sustainable economic growth. By recognizing the role of central banks in money creation, policymakers can implement targeted measures to mitigate the effects of financial crises and recessions, thereby enhancing overall economic resilience.

Additionally, debunking Ayn Rand's assertion underscores the interconnectedness of fiscal and monetary policies. Understanding the intricacies of money creation highlights the need for coordination between fiscal and monetary authorities to achieve macroeconomic goals. This recognition emphasizes the importance of coherent policy frameworks that align fiscal and monetary actions to foster sustainable economic development and mitigate distortions in the financial system.

In conclusion, the debunking of Ayn Rand's claim regarding money creation carries far-reaching implications for economic theory and policy. By dispelling misconceptions and gaining a deeper understanding of the complexities of money creation, economists, policymakers, and Objectivists can foster more nformed deliberations and implement more effective economic policies, ltimately contributing to enhanced economic prosperity and stability.

.3: Addressing Objectivist Views on Money Creation

n addressing Objectivist views on money creation, it is essential to delve into Ayn and's philosophy and challenge the assertions made in relation to the creation of money. Ayn Rand, the founder of Objectivism, argued that money is created by the productivity and effort of workers. While it is true that the value of money ;, in part, derived from the production and labor that underpins the economy, he process of money creation is a complex and multifaceted system that extends beyond individual labor. It involves the actions of central banks, commercial banks, and the broader financial system.

Objectivism emphasizes the virtues of selfishness and rational self-interest, uggesting that individuals should act in pursuit of their own happiness and well-being. These principles inform Rand's stance on money creation, wherein she posits that money is a representation of an individual's productive effort and herefore should not be subjected to government regulation. However, while ndividual effort and productivity certainly contribute to the economy, the creation and regulation of money is a function that transcends the efforts of any ingle worker or group of workers.

n reality, money creation involves the activities of central banks and the banking ystem. Central banks, such as the Federal Reserve in the United States, play a pivotal role in the creation and regulation of money. Through mechanisms such as open market operations and setting interest rates, central banks influence the money supply, which in turn affects economic activity. Commercial banks also contribute to money creation through the process of fractional reserve banking, wherein they are able to lend out a portion of deposits while holding a fraction in reserve. This process effectively expands the money supply and is a significar factor in the creation of money within the economy.

In challenging Objectivist views on money creation, it is crucial to recognize tho the financial system operates on a set of intricate mechanisms that exten beyond the efforts of individual workers. While productivity and labor ar certainly fundamental to economic prosperity, the creation and regulation c money involve a complex interplay of central banking policies, commercic bank activities, and broader market forces. By understanding an acknowledging these dynamics, it becomes evident that money creation is nc solely contingent upon the efforts of individual workers, but rather is shaped by comprehensive set of economic and financial factors. This perspective provide a more comprehensive understanding of the complexities involved in mone creation, offering a counterpoint to the Objectivist assertion that money is solek a product of individual labor.

6.4: Moving Towards a More Comprehensive Understanding a Money Creation

In this section, we will explore the implications of debunking Ayn Rand's clair about money creation and discuss the necessity of moving towards a mor comprehensive understanding of this fundamental economic concept. Th prevailing misconception promoted by Rand that money is created by workers i not only erroneous but also detrimental to a proper understanding of th complex mechanisms underlying money creation.

First and foremost, debunking Rand's claim is crucial for economists policymakers, and individuals striving to comprehend the intricate process c money creation. By dismantling this fallacy, we pave the way for a mor accurate understanding of the role of central banks, commercial banks, and the tricate interplay between fiscal and monetary policy. A comprehensive understanding of money creation is indispensable for formulating effective monetary policies, regulating the banking sector, and ensuring financial stability.

Furthermore, debunking Ayn Rand's claim is of great significance to Objectivists due to the philosophical and ideological ramifications of her assertion. Objectivism emphasizes rational self-interest and laissez-faire capitalism, and as such, a flawed understanding of money creation could lead to misguided economic principles and policies. By advocating for a more comprehensive understanding of money creation, Objectivists can align their economic perspectives with empirical evidence and sound economic reasoning, thereby strengthening their ideological framework.

In light of the aforementioned implications, it becomes evident that moving towards a more comprehensive understanding of money creation is imperative for fostering economic literacy and informed decision-making. This entails promoting educational initiatives, conducting rigorous research, and fostering dialogue among economists, policymakers, and Objectivists to enhance their understanding of money creation and its pivotal role in the functioning of modern economies.

Moreover, a more comprehensive understanding of money creation necessitates an exploration of the quantitative aspects of monetary expansion and contraction. This includes delving into statistical data on money supply, credit creation, and the impact of monetary policy on inflation, interest rates, and economic growth. By employing empirical evidence and quantitative analysis, economists and policymakers can gain deeper insights into the dynamics of money creation and its implications for macroeconomic performance.

In conclusion, debunking Ayn Rand's claim about money creation not only dispels a misleading notion but also underscores the importance of cultivating a more comprehensive understanding of this pivotal economic concept. This entails addressing the misconceptions perpetuated by Rand, acknowledging the philosophical implications for Objectivists, and delving into the quantitative aspects of money creation. As we strive towards a more comprehensive understanding, we pave the way for informed economic discourse and enlightened decision-making, thereby contributing to a more robust and well informed economic landscape.

www.ingramcontent.com/pod-product-compliance
Lightning Source LLC
Chambersburg PA
CBHW071015290526
45795CB00005B/1815